SANTA FE
Houses & Gardens

SANTA FE
Houses & Gardens

Sue Daley · Steve Gross

with an introduction by
Lucy R. Lippard

RIZZOLI
NEW YORK

First published in the United States of America in 2002 by
RIZZOLI INTERNATIONAL PUBLICATIONS, INC.
300 Park Avenue South, New York, NY 10010

ISBN: 0-8478-2475-6
LCCN: 2002090782

2002 2003 2004 2005 2006 / 10 9 8 7 6 5 4 3 2 1

Front cover: Ramona Scholder house
Back cover: West & Myerson house and garden
Page 1: A prehistoric pot in the Schenck collection
Page 2: Cave dwellings at Bandelier National Monument
Page 5: The San Jose Church in the village of Las Trampas
Pages 8–9: A landscape near Chimayo
Page 10: A doorway on Canyon Road
Page 13: The interior courtyard of the La Fonda Hotel
Page 14: A ruin in Galisteo
Page 17: The "Tent Rocks," natural volcanic formations
        at Cochiti Pueblo
Pages 18–19: Lightning over Galisteo
Page 21: The Archbishop Lamy Chapel in Tesuque
Page 22: A holy picture at the Rodriguez house
Page 24: Beehive ovens at Taos Pueblo
Page 29: An adobe wall along Canyon Road
Page 30: Roses at dusk on the high road to Taos
Page 33: A cactus bloom and barn near Dixon

Design: Judy Geib and Aldo Sampieri
Project Editor: Kristen Schilo

Distributed to the U.S. trade by St. Martin's Press

Printed and bound in China

Contents

Inside Santa Fe

by Lucy R. Lippard

When Anglos encountered the city of Santa Fe in the early nineteenth century, they were disappointed. They saw it as a group of mud hovels waiting for civilization (later arrivals were more sensitive and nostalgic, and noted approvingly that the mud houses looked as though they had risen from the earth). Today Santa Fe is idealized for the natural beauty of its desert/mountain setting, its organically winding streets and adobe compounds, the visible traces of its long history and its supposed tricultural harmony. At the same time, Santa Fe is denigrated for its enforced architectural homogeneity, its upscale overlay, self-conscious quaintness and commercial preoccupations. Both attitudes are justified. Like everywhere else, the "City Different" is many places, some of which are totally familiar to any contemporary American and some of which take on a Third- or other-worldly ambiance for those unfamiliar with the southwest.

When visitors go on about the "Land of Enchantment," it's necessary to remind them that this is one of the poorest states in the union. For most of its modern life, Santa Fe has looked backward, with all the advantages and drawbacks of both senses of the word—reliance on history and fear of change. Yet even as

newcomers roll their eyes about the inconvenient aspects of a vestigially traditional society, we are seduced by the place's charm and the historical continuity that informs it. The ancestors of the Pueblo people selling jewelry to tourists under the portal of the Palace of the Governors (built by the Spanish in 1610 on the site of a Tewa town) occupied that Palace after the Pueblo Revolt banished the invaders in 1680.

And Santa Fe, the unlikely state capital, which because of its altitude got left off the railway when it came through in 1880, epitomizes this "land of contrasts" image. Santa Fe is not typical of New Mexico cities, in part because it is the rest of the world's "fanta-se" (or, more uncharitably, "Santa Fake"). Residents tend to be torn between its very real beauty, rooted in traditions that remain important even as they are rapidly disappearing and the destruction of its small-town scale by the hordes of outsiders crowding the narrow streets. Over the last twenty years, the mix has been augmented by transplants from all over the United States, some of whom demand an intimacy that is elitist rather than communal, and some of whom build seldom-used trophy houses that blight the surrounding hilltops. As Chris Wilson has written in his groundbreaking book, *The Myth of Santa Fe: Creating a Modern Regional Tradition*: "Can a community sustain immigration of 1 percent per year and a steady visitor population of 4 percent? The answer depends on the vitality of the local culture, on the conditions of the interactions of native residents with visitors and newcomers, and on the willingness of everyone to put aside stereotypes and open themselves to real communication."

Santa Fe is still a small city, under 65,000 people, although the surrounding county has boomed to a similar population, all of which shops in Santa Fe. It is easy to get around, and hard to find your way around. You can still be startled by dirt roads near the Plaza, and the occasional patch of rural landscape in the inner city—once farmed—that is still fed water by a "lateral" (a branch of the mother ditch or *acequia madre*). If authenticity is out of our reach, historical memory is not. Thus the ambivalence that characterizes many residents' emotions about their place.

From the outside, since statehood was achieved in 1912 and a failing economy was reinvented for tourism through the adoption of a hybrid Pueblo/Spanish Revival, Santa Fe's built environment keeps a low profile, dictated by law. There are few "great buildings" that stand out like those of Chicago or New York. It was actually planned that way as early as the sixteenth century, when King Philip II of Spain laid down the law that New World settlements should be based in architectural homogeneity "for the sake of beauty." Santa Fe's central plaza was transformed from a Tewa pueblo to a low, mudbrick Spanish garrison, a Tewa pueblo again (for twelve years), a Mexican provincial town, and then an American territorial marketplace,

complete with pitched tin roofs and neo-eastern trims. In 1912 it was returned to something vaguely—very vaguely—resembling its origins, forgetting the "humble" part. The "City Different" rubric appeared at the same time, with the creation of the "New-Old Santa Fe" we now know. Preservation, restoration and reinvention became the tools of design control, a process cemented in the mid-1950s (and updated in the 1980s) with the "Historical Styles Ordinance." Thanks to these decrees, merely repairing a roof in the historic district can be a laborious, expensive, and delicate political task.

In terms of national education, the history of New Mexico has been severed from that of the rest of the United States, an error that adds to its present reputation for exoticism. Santa Fe follows St. Augustine, Florida as the nation's second "oldest city," and claims the "longest continuously used building." English-over-Spanish hierarchy has prevailed in our history books, despite the fact that both of these out-of-the-way cities were settled long before the northeastern sites schoolchildren learn to call the cradle of North American civilization. What we call "prehistory" belongs to indigenous peoples (as though no one had a history until Europeans could write it down their way). Colonial history in the area belongs to Spain and Mexico. "Americans" only arrived in strength in the 1840s, and only after the Civil War consolidated their population on the land taken

from Mexico, breaking the 1848 treaty of Guadalupe Hidalgo and casually appropriating property others had fought and lived hard for over the previous centuries.

Externally, everyone shares Santa Fe's general ambiance: acres of adobe and stucco imitations, downtown charm and congestion, the monotonous commercialization of the Cerrillos Road strip and the merciless traffic on St. Francis drive. Architecturally, it's all the same and all different. No two houses are truly identical despite the overall visual unity, with the exception of the ubiquitous new condos, although cultural markers remain persistent, photographs of exterior Santa Fe by a postcard photographer and a skilled picture thinker look very much the same. Clichés rule. The "place" is softly dominant, hard to manipulate, immediately readable and quite opaque.

Interiors are another story. Houses are Santa Fe's treasures, the intimate sites of lives lived in and out of the public eye. They are tantalizing walled or tucked-away sanctuaries envied and imagined by visitors. Some are sprawling and even grandiose, but the scale is rarely baronial, unlike the giant structures being built in the surrounding countryside. Steve Gross and Sue Daley have selected an intriguing cross-section of *homes*, managing for the most part to avoid the depredations of "Santa Fe style," which threaten to make everything as homogenous inside as outside. Their choices offer an interesting case study of the

intersection of photography and lifestyle, both belying and reinforcing the Santa Fe stereotypes. (Actually, several of these houses are not in Santa Fe but within a wide radius of villages from Galisteo to Coyote, each of which, it should be noted, has its own history separate from and often highly divergent from that of the capital.) Different eras are evoked—from the nineteenth century to the 1950s or 1990s—and personal styles always make up the difference. In a few cases the illustrious inhabitant remains in residence.

Many of the houses photographed for this book were once modest, built by earlier settlers or economically challenged artists. For instance, Ramona Scholder's house in Galisteo (built by the Epifanio Mora family around 1880), retains an aura of traditional graciousness, in part because of its owner's talents and in part because of its setting in an old village that is decidedly gentrified but retains much of its original character. Some private residences have since been remodeled within an inch of their lives. Others, like Myrtle Stedman's lovely old place, retain some of the worn simplicity that comes from a genuine admiration for traditional lifestyles of the less than rich. J.B. Jackson, the brilliant writer on landscape and the vernacular, who shared these values, could have produced one of his crystal clear essays on the transformation of his former home in La Cienega.

Such houses in Santa Fe may still be known, and even

plaqued, as the "Vierra house," "the Paloheimo/Curtin house," or the "Vigil house"—names that are regionally famous in Santa Fe's history. (It is necessary to learn a whole new art history when one moves to the southwest.) These homes are of interest less for their architectural features, as their recent history. They also accrue value from the cultural icons who live or once lived there, from the elusive traces of their talents and personalities. Mary and Chuck Kehoe's home, for instance, was built by the late artist and local hero Bill Lumpkins, who pioneered a modern usage of solar/adobe. Mabel Dodge Luhan's Taos house is now an inn. Bishop Lamy's Chapel is on the grounds of a resort. Randall Davey's home (originally the Candelario Martinez house) is on an Audubon reserve, open to the public with some of its original furnishings.

The home of the highly respected WPA painter and straw appliqué artist Eliseo and Paula Rodriguez is part of a traditional continuum that others are imitating. The Rodriguez's house, as photographed, is both elegant and actually "homey." Hardly lacking in beautiful objects, it nevertheless sits comfortably in its place and in the culture it helps to create. The "barrio and bottle gardens" included here are of a genre that deserves a book on its own. Suffice it to say that their inventiveness—also based on found materials—depends not on history, nor on provenance, but on ongoing creativity in the accumulative mode associated with much vernacular art.

A number of the owners or former owners of these homes

are artists, with whom the photographers obviously feel an affinity. The interiors shown often appear as carefully composed as a canvas might be. Other homeowners are scholars, collectors and art dealers, and they too compose their own sets, as we all do. Despite the heavy hand of New Mexico on most of these interiors, it is clear that we transplants (and in the greater scheme of things that includes those who arrived decades and even centuries ago) bring our own cultural and geographical baggage with us. The rooms in which we live are as eclectic as the city itself. They are layered with illegible personal narratives, open to the viewer's interpretation.

The "traditional look" of most of these houses is not factually traditional. It is a recreated tradition—some would say an imagined tradition—compatible with the tastes of those who own the dwellings. Reconstruction of the past remains a pleasurable, though hardly an "authentic" pastime. Ruskin called restoration (as opposed to preservation) a matter of "the most total destruction a building can suffer." Yet we must assume that these interiors are "authentic" to the inhabitants and their individual histories, their undisclosed lives, desires and accomplishments. Yet few inhabitants, native or "just off the bus"—do not covet Santa Fe's material culture. Many of the homes featured in this book display extraordinarily shaped and painted indigenous pots; stunning Navajo and Chimayo weavings; sober old *bultos*, *Santos*, and *retablos*; floral *colchas*; intricately carved *trasteros*; and ingeniously simple tinwork and baskets, silver and turquoise, beadwork and textiles. And everywhere the local treasures are mixed with exquisite oddities from around the world (Moroccan and Mexican seem particularly popular in this group) that seem compatible with centuries of local production. Some of these homes might easily be museums.

Some of the owners probably acquired their precious objects long ago when times were particularly hard and they were being sold cheap. Some came by them more personally, as gifts from the makers or trades of artwork for artwork. Some continue to buy them at increasingly astronomical prices. And there is no one, not even the most critical mind in the state, who does not on some level envy those living daily among these objects. Though sadly they are artifacts of the lost heritages of other southwestern cultures, they are also among the most beautiful human-made objects in the world.

While some of these interiors might be models for interior decorators, there are fascinating anomalies—an artist's cliff-side cave in Coyote, with its rough stone walls and textured decorations; a "sandcastle" in Aqua Fria; a domed private chapel; a New York art dealer's pristine new home with the chairs arranged like sculptures; a handprint on the white wall of a fireplace. Unique in its double identity is the atypically small apartment of a contemporary artist who lives in El Zaguan, the home of the Historic

Santa Fe Foundation on Canyon Road—a winding, uphill street that has become the epitome of combined art, wealth and tourism. Martha DeFoe makes "chamber works" by transforming her two rooms into minimal/conceptual art, Zen-like in its serendipitous simplicity. The clean, spare, intellectual content of her living quarters changes a few times a year. The sculpture/furniture therein is formed of materials found in the neighborhood, at the Rios Lumber Yard, for instance, which supplies the east side with firewood; others come from friends or have been discarded at the Canyon Road curb. There is a nice irony to this idiosyncratic artwork/artist's home hidden away within the bastion of historical Santa Fe. DeFoe's apartment coexists with and counteracts all the obligatory Santa Fe Style clichés and, in a curious way, echoes the clarity and simplicity of "the real Santa Fe." This home is "authentic"—it tries to be nothing that it isn't because it is art.

"It is more gracious, somehow, to be poor in an adobe house," is a sentiment presumably once common in Santa Fe's artists' colony (as expressed by Edna Robertson and Sarah Nestor in their book *Artists of the Canyons and Caminos*). So long as the design ordinances hold, Santa Fe's identity will be inseparable from adobe, mud plaster and stucco imitations thereof. No material is more sensuous or more suggestive of the human touch and of the work of the *enjarradora*—the traditional, and almost extinct, female plasterer who works with her hands, caressing the walls and leaving her imprint on them. (Zennia Victor's and Gaylon Duke's bedroom brings this process to mind.) The rough and smooth textures of mud and stone can be contrasted, augmented by old woods, by the ubiquitous books, paintings, tiles, the *nichos* and deep sills waiting for a saint or a pot of flowers.

Light, color and surface sustain the photographers in this kind of work. Daley's and Gross's previous books testify to their skill in catching the right angle, the right surface, the right detail and the right time of day to bring out the effect that most impresses them. Their task is to make the views as striking as possible and to add a certain depth—to provide insights into the way the actual spaces can be experienced. Like most of the readers/viewers of this book, I've been in few of these homes, so I too am a voyeur, submitting to the sights seen through the photographers' eyes, the sites described by their bodies moving through space. The overall impression that is so telling when we enter any room is not available to still photographers. They give us a collage that we must glue together in our mind's eye, a collage that is tantalizingly fragmented and momentary, a collage that is likely to spawn a whole new generation of would-be New Mexicans.

Randall Davey Historic House

page 34

The arched gate and stone steps lead to the courtyard of artist Randall Davey's former painting studio on Upper Canyon Road.

◀

pages 36–37

Murals painted by Randall Davey on the pink-stucco exterior include fanciful depictions of burros, which used to traverse the old sheep herding trails following along the Santa Fe River in the canyon below the house. Davey bought the house in 1920 and turned it into his family residence, where he lived and worked until his death in 1964. It is now part of the Audubon Society.

right

Davey's painting studio remains very much the way he left it. An avid hunter and polo player, he was noted for his portraits of jockeys and racetrack scenes. Along with his mentor, Robert Henri, and friend John Sloan, Davey was influential in the development of the new American Realism style at the turn of the last century, and believed in painting what he saw in everyday life. The woman in the red dress is his second wife, Isabel.

page 40

The second floor sala *has a white wooden staircase carved by a local artisan. Davey, who studied architecture at Cornell, redesigned the house himself, creating larger and sunnier rooms. Prominent members of the Santa Fe arts community, he and his wife Isabel often entertained in their music and book-filled home.*

page 41

On a bedroom door off the sala, *Davey painted two piñon jays inside the intricately carved star-shaped design.*

right

A nude portrait of Isabel hangs next to a very tall early Victorian gilded mirror on the sala wall. Davey often painted geraniums, one of the favorite flowers of New Mexico. The flowers are still found in big clay pots in nearly every window of the house.

left

The sitting room on the first floor was used as a reception area where Davey often entertained his guests by playing the cello. The furnishings are a mix of some of the Victorian objects he brought with him from New York City, and the Spanish Colonial and rustic New Mexican pieces he found locally.

page 46

In Isabel's dressing room, Davey painted an exotic and sensual Gauguin-like mural as a surprise for her while she was away on a trip. The wooden floor planks were painted to imitate black and white tiles, which were considered very chic in the 1940s.

page 47

The atmospheric illusion is further enhanced by the row of arched mirrors set into carved closet doors that line one wall of the dressing room. A little yellow slipper chair sits close to the brick-lined corner fireplace.

urand
Garden

page 48

An ancient French iceberg shrub rose called "White Cascade" is one of the historic plants found in the front garden of Albert and Connie Durand, who like to use heirloom varieties of roses rather than the newer hybrids.

left

The Durands hand-built their organically curved adobe on Canyon Road using traditional techniques, allowing the lines of the house to follow the contours of the cliff edge on which it sits. The sloping garden wall and archway are reminiscent of the massive buttressing of New Mexican mission churches. A wooden ladder is used to reach the roof where sunset-viewing parties are held.

right top

A "Dynamite" climbing rose with lush red velvet blossoms is supported by one of the hand-carved, curved columns of the portal. The Durands wanted to create a "cottage garden" in keeping with the informal way gardens evolved in Santa Fe.

right bottom

A window set into the privacy wall surrounding the house frames another "White Cascade" rose bush.

Myrtle Stedman House

page 52

The house called "Cottonwoods" was built by artists Myrtle and Wilfred Stedman, with the help of their two boys, during the years of World War II. It sits on several acres of oats and alfalfa fields in the village of Tesuque. The Stedmans first came upon Tesuque on one of their painting expeditions from Texas during the Depression, and decided to settle here amid the old apple orchards started by Alsatian gardeners in the 1860s.

page 54

Myrtle told her husband "Sted" that she wanted "to build a house stretched out like a lizard in the sun, with big windows for the sun and light to come in." The large vigas *are salvaged utility poles, skinned with a drawknife by ten-year-old son Wilfred. The Stedmans rescued the big wooden table from their neighborhood restaurant El Nido, the place where local artists gathered to drink and dance.*

page 55

A Chimayo blanket, done in traditional colors, hangs on a wall above a simple wood chest whose sunflowers were carved in by Sted. The arrangement of objects here shows the look of studied naturalness that Myrtle prizes.

right

A former broom closet has been transformed into a sanctuary. To Myrtle, the cross indicates "the power and constructive creation, the mating sign of the ancients and the sign of planting."

Myrtle Stedman House 57

left top

A kitchen door was painted by Myrtle to depict scenes of her life in Tesuque. The lawn tractor on the top panel represents one that her son Tom built from scratch.

left bottom

The humble kitchen is an example of Myrtle's love of true simplicity, which, she says, "in no way describes an imbecilic or artsy approach, but one of grace and economy." When hardware was scarce during the war years, Myrtle and Sted fashioned the drawer-pulls out of pieces of leather and wood.

right

Over the guest bed hang two of Myrtle's paintings. Besides her artwork and poetry, she is well known as a building contractor, designer of, and authority on adobe homes and New Mexican rural architecture.

Mary & Chuck Kehoe House

page 60

Mary Kehoe's father, who was a Louisiana cattle rancher, left her his hand-tooled leather saddle, which has his brand and name engraved on it. Set out on her patio, it's surrounded by Mexican cowboy hats from the 1940s and '50s.

page 62

A sunny, geranium filled entrance hall was part of the artist/architect Bill Lumpkins's original 1960s passive-solar design for the house, which present owners Mary and Chuck Kehoe call "post-pueblo modern." An American Deco burl sideboard supports some of the 1930s Mexican silver that Mary collects. In a vintage silver tureen, two cacti have been grafted together to create a "designer" cactus.

page 63

The central patio and courtyard area is used year round by the Kehoes. Built-in bancos, upon which Bailey the dog reclines, are covered in rugs and tapestries that change with the seasons. The view from here looks north to the piñon and juniper covered Sangre de Cristo Mountains.

right

Double arches lead from the dining room to the red living room. An adobe fireplace was shaped into a corner and decorated with pretty little Mexican tiles. Moroccan pillows from the Santa Fe flea market are scattered about, along with African beaded chieftain chairs and baskets.

left

The Kehoe kitchen used to be "the most boring part of the house," says Mary until she began painting the cabinets one night and permanently installed the Christmas lights, creating this very cool and funky room. Retro oilcloths cover the table while inexpensive Saltillo blankets hide the cereal boxes.

page 68

Mary painted the walls of the dining room in her signature ochre yellow color. The coved ceiling, corbels and lintels are some of the original Lumpkins' details that came with the house.

▶▶
page 69

On the patio, two red, carved African gourds sit next to botanical candles. The green Mexican plates are glued to the wall and are part of a huge set given to Mary by her mother. They are grouped around an enormous Turkish copper banquet pan that, Mary says, is "too large to ever use."

Ford Ruthling

House and Garden

page 70

Artist Ford Ruthling, a native New Mexican who grew up in Tesuque, now makes his home in a vibrantly landscaped sprawling compound of four buildings in the South Capital area of Santa Fe. On the elegant portal overlooking the courtyard, a Taos daybed and a wrought iron table from the flea market provide the setting for Ford's breakfasts. Hung in a row above a processional banner from a French Catholic church are some of the "harvest bowls" Ford designs.

page 72

A shockingly rich profusion of colors is found throughout Ford's lavish landscape where delphiniums flourish next to red and white poppies. The garden contains many of the old apricot and cherry trees that were planted around the time the house was first built in 1907.

page 73

Along one wall of this conservatory room, Ford built a window out of some bull's eye glass medallions that he commissioned to be made in Mexico forty years ago. The decorative carved screen opens out to allow cooling breezes to circulate over the primitive Mexican bench. A huge green and white bowl from Spain sits upon a huipil *table.*

right

The conservatory has a translucent ceiling made of corrugated panels. Dinner parties are held here under the Indian umbrella in winter when the room is full of plants. The tin and glass stars and crosses are garden lights designed by Ford, made to hold lit candles inside.

◀◀

page 76

Furnished with obvious joy, the library is at ease with New Mexican traditions. Landscape paintings and portraits mix with pueblo pots and reliquaries. An "old man dance mask" made from a single piece of wood in Mexico lights the room from above. A santo from Peru rests within an ornate gold gessoed colonial frame above the brick fireplace.

◀

page 77

A shelf above the twin "linenfold" carved guest beds holds some of the nichos Ford has been collecting since "the time when you could pick them up at garage sales for nothing." After years of repairing old nichos and becoming fascinated by their intricate designs, Ford eventually began to make his own.

right

Ford says he has used very little restraint in his garden design. "It's obscene to see so many colors at one time," he says. The glass garden lights are set into blue ceramic Mexican pots filled with carnations. Behind them, a carved goat and rabbit cavort in a "folly" Ford made with twisted wood columns and festive iron awnings.

Duke - Victor House

page 80
A wooden observation deck off the bedroom overlooks the Arroyo Hondo, Spanish for "deep canyon."

left

Like a sandcastle situated on the southern edge of Santa Fe, Zennia Victor and Gaylon Duke's fantastically shaped adobe sprang from their imaginations as much as from local building traditions. Zennia and Gaylon, who are world travelers and educators, used the traditional native "hand puddling" technique of adobe building.

right

Ladder stairs lead up to a "shepherd's bed" built above a wood burning stove. Zennia Victor, inspired by the Bandelier Monument pictographs, painted stylized human and animal figures along the edge of the loft bed. The low wall of adobe bricks divides the open space floor plan.

page 86

In the kitchen area of the main room, lamps made out of baskets and dried gourds hang above counters constructed of oak, tiles and marble salvaged from a bank in Albuquerque. Zennia and Victor obtained a permit from the National Forest to cut spruce and pine trees for the large ceiling vigas.

page 87

The lower level bedroom was created by digging out the hillside and then using the displaced earth to build the walls upstairs. The blue plastered adobe gives one "the feeling as though you're floating in the sky when you're lying on the bed, looking out over the arroyo," says Zennia. A ladder from the Philippines was once used for climbing from one rice paddy to another.

right

At the entrance gate, a brass bell serves as a counterweight and also rings when the door is opened. Everyone has their own personal theory as to why doors and windows are so often painted blue in New Mexico. Zennia and Gaylon say it's because the blue repels mosquitoes and evil spirits. The Tibetan flags send out prayers each time they flutter in the breeze.

Rodriguez House

◀◀

page 90

Paula Rodriguez has always kept carefully arranged altars above her fireplaces. Two of Paula's "poor man's gold," or straw appliqué scenes of the Blessed Virgin Mary hang on the wall.

right

A floor of Colorado flagstone covers the two levels of the sala *in the home of Paula and Eliseo Rodriguez. The rugs and many of their pots were collected over the years, starting in the 1930s on visits to pueblos and the annual Indian Market. Eliseo cut, carved and finished the elegant* vigas. *He learned one of the secrets of building a corner fireplace by making a small egg shaped bump at the back that would help draw up the smoke.*

left

In their patio garden, Eliseo and Paula constructed an arch out of chicken wire and cement. The two artists began building their own house in 1936 on land that belonged to Eliseo's father on a hillside above Canyon Road. The adobe they made "had no formal plan, it just slowly evolved over many years from the soil and the trees and our bare hands." Today the high stone walls barely contain the lush overgrown garden, full of flowers, fruit trees and grapevines.

page 96

A still life arrangement in the living room contains two of Eliseo's paintings. His work, such as this powerful crucifixion scene, shows the combination of his cultural heritage and personal religious beliefs. In the 1940s Eliseo found employment making stained glass, altars and religious paintings for churches in the Southwest.

page 97

Eliseo has been a painter for over seventy years and had a close association with the Cinco Pintores' artist's enclave living around the corner from him in his early days. The black and white photo is by another former neighbor and friend, the photographer Laura Gilpin.

page 98–99

In a sunny, plant filled corner of the sitting room rests one of Eliseo's straw appliqué crosses. He learned and revived the old Hispanic art form of creating "paintings in straw" from the WPA work program for artists. The technique, which dates back to the days of the Moors in Spain, had been in danger of disappearing.

right

On the wall hang a reverse painted retablo, an angel on wood and a painting of San Pasqual, the patron saint of cooking. Like much of Eliseo's work, these reflect his fascination with the lives of the saints.

M West&yerson

House and Garden

page 102

The Cerro Gordo compound of Cynthia West, an artist, poet and potter, and Reno Myerson, a healer and bodyworker, consists of several colorful buildings and acres of carefully tended gardens. The 150-year-old house once belonged to the Luhan family, who planted many peach trees, raised goats and grew herbs, which they then sold to local curanderos.

above

Affixed to a latia, or coyote fence is a Guadalupe image given to Cynthia and Reno by a healer friend. The cedar, fir or aspen-poled fences were constructed for privacy and design, as much as for deterring any marauding coyotes from snitching sheep.

right

The compound, called "the Bohemian Embassy," has been well known as an arts and healing center for many years. The firepit is used to heat up rocks for a tented sweat lodge. The dome shape of the chapel Cynthia built is seen in the distance.

page 106

In an El Paso taco stand one day, Cynthia saw an apparition of the Virgin of Guadalupe, who asked her to build a chapel for Her. To that end, Cynthia enlisted the help of a Mexican craftsman, who possessed the secret of how to build a freestanding dome without any supports. The intimate and serene space contains a fireplace, floral offerings and low meditation benches.

page 107

The kitchen table is "the center of the cyclone and the place where many great ideas and projects have been conceived." Cynthia and Reno put in the traditional "shepherd's fireplace" so that the fire would be just at eye level when seated at table. Wild columbines that grow in great profusion here fill the stoneware jar that Cynthia made.

right

Black and white Buddha heads are found in the terraced garden that slopes down to fields once farmed by the Indians. Cynthia, Reno and their friends dug out and re-instated "miles of the hundreds-of-years-old acequias that watered the Hispanic milpas, corn, and bean fields."

Curtin-Paloheimo House

page 110

In the late 1920s, Leonora Scott Muse Curtin built this well-proportioned Territorial style house on several acres of land on Acequia Madre Street. Tall blue spruce and cottonwood trees tower over chamisa bushes and the abundant hardy yellow roses that Leonora, an avid gardener, planted.

left top

In this long sala, many of the artists and writers of Leonora Curtin's day were entertained and known to "get wild." Among them were the poet Witter Bynner, artist Olive Rush, the painters Sheldon Parsons, Will Schuster and Marsden Hartley, and writer Mary Austin.

left bottom

The screen at the entrance to the dining room was painted by Leonora Curtin's mother, Eva Feynes. The Curtin women collected paintings and artwork, including the portrait hanging above the door of an Indian man, done by Joseph Henry Sharp.

right

A corner of the sala was a place to take afternoon tea while seated upon the early Jacobean settle. Leonora Curtin catalogued the traditional uses of Southwestern plants and healing herbs in numerous books on ethnobiology. Traveling about the region, she visited Indian and Hispanic homes to collect and preserve the area's herbal knowledge. Her library shelves also contain a large number of cowboy westerns and books by local authors.

right

Spanish market trunks are found at the foot of each twin bed in the "white bedroom." During the Depression, Leonora Paloheimo and her mother, Leonora Curtin, helped start the Spanish Market in Santa Fe as a way of encouraging the production of local crafts by providing a place for artists to sell their work. Above the radiators, displayed artifacts include a parfleche, Hopi and Apache baskets, and African figures, all gathered on their travels.

page 116

The Curtin women hired a craftsman to execute the twisted stone columns around the fireplace in the sala. *On a wrought iron coat rack hang various implements, such as a skeleton key, fork, spoons and a strainer, all handed down in the family. A Spanish* bulto *of Our Lady of Mt. Carmel sits atop the mantel.*

page 117

In the gaily painted sewing room with sawtooth trim, cabinets line the walls and contain stored linens. The walls are believed to have been painted by artist Eva Feynes. Eva Paloheimo, Feynes's great-granddaughter, remembers ironing and sewing being done in this room.

Barrio and Bottle Gardens

page 118

The extraordinarily colorful garden created by Mary Helen and Charles Sharpe on Agua Fria St. has grown over 31 years. Working together, and possessing an unusual knack for coaxing large and vigorous blooms from the dry sandy soil, the Sharpes, who love all sorts of roses, have "shifted to plastic" in the last few years to help conserve water.

left top

In the garden where "everything has a little story behind it" a statue of St Francis has been placed facing the front door in honor of the patron saint of the city. Mary Helen and Charles, who admit to having a bit of an artistic side, like to "check out and find inspiring stuff everywhere and then haul it home." Most of the numerous statues and planters have been hand-painted by Helen.

left bottom

In another barrio garden, different types of planters offer stylistic variations as well as a more hospitable soil mix. In times of water rationing, artificial flowers are the predominant blossoms. Coral and turquoise, two traditional New Mexican colors, are used to highlight the architecture of the space.

right

This small parking lot has been transformed into an imaginative sculpture garden using cinderblocks, adobe and a combination of natural and recycled objects. The gnarly qualities of tree roots are enhanced with river rocks and an accent of chainlink trim.

left

A cross of bottlenecks threaded with bailing wire hang on the fence of this folkloric bottle garden along Highway 14. The accumulation of hundreds of bottles, many dating to the 1800s, is a colorful catalog of the tinctures, tonics and libations used in the town of Golden during the boom years of gold and silver mining.

right top

Trees hung with bottles to trap and ward off evil spirits have been documented in the U.S. for more than a century. After years of being exposed to the intense New Mexican sun, many clear bottles achieve an amethyst tint.

right bottom

Bleached bones are woven into a section of the fence and topped off with telephone pole insulators in this garden of random archeology.

Ramona
Scholder
House and Garden

page 124

In the quaint and dusty village of Galisteo, Ramona Scholder inhabits the ancient Mora Hacienda, which dates from the time of the first Spanish land grant in the town. Ramona says she "never wanted to build my own dream house," and prefers to live in this stately old house that has been lived in many, many times before. The red painted open shelving and under-the- counter fireplace were both added to the kitchen by Ramona.

page 126

The buffalo head in Ramona's living room came from one of the Fred Harvey Houses, which were restaurants built along the Santa Fe railroad to attract tourists to the Southwest in the 1880s. A previous owner, Major Felton, a 1930s art-deco illustrator, built the fireplace mantle and much of the woodwork throughout the house.

page 127

A separate building houses a painting studio, office, guest quarters and this small library room. The bench is from an old New Mexican church and was used by priests and altar boys for resting while saying Mass.

right

Innumerable crosses, santos and a weeping Mary from Guatamala are displayed together in Ramona's bedroom. A St. Anthony of Padua statue from Spain has been placed under a wooden canopy along with St. Rocque's dog, believed to be a guardian angel in disguise.

page 130

Ramona says she "loves waking up surrounded by all these beautiful things." A painting by artist and silversmith, Karl Larsen, hangs above a small carved chair from northern New Mexico.

page 131

The rose colored checkered tile floor is part of a 1950's renovation of the guest bedroom, where a painting on paper by Fritz Scholder hangs next to a framed piece of Chinese embroidery. The green New Mexican washstand as well as the bed from "back east" both date to the early 1900s.

right

A patch of "iris ordinaire" thrives in the oasis-like garden of the walled-in compound. Ramona has created areas of shade in order to cut down on the amount of watering needed.

Douglas Johnson

Cliff Dwelling

page 134

In artist Douglas Johnson's handmade stone cliff dwelling, a 12 foot aspen wood "kiva" ladder leads down from a second story bedroom area.

page 136–7

Douglas Johnson spent time exploring and learning from the ancient Anasazi cliff dwellings on the Navajo Reservation, where he "found whole towns tucked away in caves." He began constructing this house for himself on the side of a silent and remote canyon in the Jemez Mountains in 1973. Built above a verdant creekside, the dwelling was made out of stones and adobe pine-needle bricks recycled from a nearby Hispanic ruin.

left

In the kitchen corner, the walls are made of smooth river rocks which Douglas hauled up from the streambed below. The house, which has no running water or electricity, is illuminated at night by kerosene lanterns. Part of Douglas's daily ritual involves carrying buckets of water and bundles of firewood up the steep path to the house.

page 140

On one of the rock walls hangs Douglas's collection of nichitos and retablos from Mexico, New Mexico and Peru. They depict various saints and scenarios of the Catholic religion, some with frames made of cut up tin cans. Douglas incorporates the area's Hispanic culture into his artwork, drawing upon retablos like these as well as the carved santos, Chimayo weavings and vernacular car sculptures called "low riders."

page 141

Using only hand tools, Douglas constructed the rock walls using techniques he learned by studying the "delicate mosaic-like work of Chaco Canyon and the cut block style of Mesa Verde."

142   *Douglas Johnson Cliff Dwelling*

page 142

A one hundred-year-old woodstove is used for cooking and heating in the kitchen, which is reminiscent of an old miner's camp. Douglas keeps all of his utensils and dishes in the green depression era handmade cabinet from the Midwest.

page 143

On the second story, Douglas's bed nestles against the cliff face. He says, "It's as though I had taken the cliff itself and pulled it around me like a blanket to provide shelter from the elements."

right

The sandstone wall of the second floor has been "sculpted into fantastic shapes by the wind and the rain." Set within naturally formed niches are three reddish San Juan Pueblo doughball pots, circa 1900, which "no one alive can make anymore." The train set curving along the cliffside wall is a surreal juxtaposition of scale and represents Douglas's childhood fascination with the Santa Fe railroad.

Pearl-Blum House

page 146

Set in an old apple orchard in the Big Tesuque River Valley, this flowing adobe was built in the 1960s by a silversmith, and is now the home of Dorothy Pearl and Arthur Blum, who both work in the film industry. The house, with its smooth, soft, curvilinear lines seemed to them to require "the big, beefy vigas, posts and cartoon-sized corbels" that were added on to balance the design.

left top

The ornamented living room fireplace is a much-prized detail in the house. Dorothy originally thought the blackened band around it was made of tin, but upon cleaning it "the tarnish disappeared to reveal sterling silver with huge chunks of turquoise, coral and onyx embedded in it."

left bottom

In what Dorothy calls her "Georgia O'Keeffe corner," she's placed a papier mâché vase full of red roses in lieu of a fire.

right

The dining room table came from the "Grapes of Wrath aisle" at the Tesuque flea market, as did the whimsical painting of a New Mexican church. Dorothy Pearl says she "never misses a weekend at the town flea market, which is as good as the one in Paris."

right

Pearl and Blum ripped the roof off of the small, dark, low-ceilinged kitchen and raised it two feet. The open shelves and cabinets were built in the Peñasco style with crucitas, *or little cut out crosses, carved into the woodwork. They've been painted a bright blue "to pull your eye to them and match the stools that came from Marrakech."*

DeFoe

Apartment in El Zaguan Historic House and Gardens

page 152

Martha DeFoe, an artist/designer, makes her home in an apartment in the long, rambling landmark building known as "El Zaguan" on Canyon Road. Next to her grandmother's rocking chair from Michigan, a pile of smooth black river stones awaits transformation.

left

Martha's living space, which she calls "Chamberworks," is a harmonious combination of found and recycled materials that are always changing. The long, low bench is made of a metal frame she found at the "Black Hole" salvage yard, to which she added tongue and groove flooring from an old gym. A discarded stainless steel print dryer forms the base of the glass-topped table.

right top

The zaguan, or covered passageway, contains a closet that houses Martha's refrigerator. Its doors were painted by Dorothy Stewart back when her sister Margretta Dietrich bought the building to save it from development. Lightning carved shutters hang on leather hinges and hide mailboxes behind them.

right bottom

On the bedroom wall, Martha has created a grid from pieces of hairdresser's silver foil. The arc suspended above her simple, striped palette bed is a hoop from an old covered wagon.

The picket-fenced garden at El Zaguan has a Victorian-era diamond shaped pattern that was unearthed during an archeological dig in the 1990s. The Territorial style house, which dates to the Civil War era, belonged to wealthy frontier merchant James L. Johnson, in the days when Santa Fe was a major trade center. It was renovated at a later date under the direction of Kate Chapman, who was one of the first practitioners of the Spanish and Pueblo revival styles. The garden, now open to the public, still contains two ancient horse chestnut trees, as well as antique peonies from China, wild roses and old fruit trees.

Heldman former Carlos Vierra House

page 158

The tin-lined Zuni style corner fireplace was used to heat the room when it was the studio of artist Carlos Vierra. The adobe half-wall creates a corner in the middle of the room and shelters the fire from drafts.

right top

Above the bar in the dining room hang some of present owners Gladys and Julius Heldman's collection of New Mexico paintings, including ones done by the "Cinco Pintores" group and a fall landscape by Carlos Vierra.

right bottom

In the living room, the Heldmans have kept the essential elements of Vierra's design while blending in objects from their own travels. The painted, carved vigas and rough-hewn wood lintels were designed by Vierra to reflect the Moorish roots of the New Mexican style, as well as to show the skill and beauty of hand work.

page 160

Ivy completely covers the garden side of the Heldman's adobe house.

left

Situated off the Old Pecos Trail, the handsome Pueblo-Spanish Revival house was begun in 1917 by photographer, architect, painter and archeologist Carlos Vierra. The sloping, sculptural and massive shapes, the round log columns and the wooden rain spouts are all typical of the revival style Vierra helped to create.

Mabel Dodge Luhan

Historic House and Inn

page 164

In Mabel Dodge Luhan's time, this courtyard was once a carport where she parked her Model T beside a majestic pear tree.

page 166

A combination of Spanish hacienda *and Pueblo style, this adobe house was built in 1918 for Mabel Dodge Luhan, an heiress, writer and arts patron, and her fourth husband Tony Luhan, a Taos pueblo man. The house was called Los Gallos for its rows of Mexican ceramic roosters perched along the roofline. The unusual third story contains a solarium for sunbathing.*

◀

page 167

Mabel's twenty-two room Taos estate attracted and inspired a steady stream of visiting artists, among them D.H.Lawrence. One day Lawrence and a "disciple" of his, Lady Dorothy Brett, took a bottle of wine into the bathroom and painted the colorful symbols and designs on the windows. Mabel's bath contained the first indoor plumbing in Taos.

left

The log cabin room with its rough, whitewashed walls, river-stone fireplace and Taos daybed was built for Mabel's son John, to be used as his classroom.

page 170

In traditional Spanish hacienda style, the long, shady portal links together the various parts of the sprawling adobe Mabel called her "hodgepodge of a house."

▶▶

page 171

Mabel had a native artisan build her this large bed with its oversized spiral posts, which match the ropas, columns that look like twisted ropes. It is so massive that it had to be carved on site and cannot be removed from her former bedroom.

Erhard former John Sloan House

page 172

The living room of Doris and Louis Erhard's home is part of the original house called "Sin Agua" built in 1940 by painter John Sloan. Sloan, who was one of the American realist "Ashcan School" painters, began coming to Santa Fe in 1919 to spend the summers, and worked to help preserve the character and original look of the town.

left top

Doris, who is an anthropologist, and Louis, an archeologist, are both "intensely interested in the material culture of the Near East and North Africa." They've picked up many of their furnishings at souks, bazaars and markets on their travels and expeditions, like this coffee pot from Oman.

left bottom

The tower bedroom has a Navajo hogan type ceiling made of diagonally overlapped vigas and latillas.

right

In the entrance hall, a colonial chest from Goa, window grilles from Afghanistan, and a leather ottoman from Morocco are all in the mix with Salvation Army lamps that Doris's father found in Rochester in the 1940s.

Sallie Wagner House

page 176

Sallie Wagner's dining room fireplace has a handprint on it made by the Pueblo Indian woman who built it.

left

Sallie moved to this house in the 1950s after running a trading post called "Wide Ruins" on the Navajo reservation. The carved turquoise screen door is typical of the region.

right

Above the courtyard of the Wagner house is a separate building called the "mirador," meaning a place with a view. The rustic building has windows made out of the windshields of old sedans.

left top

"I like the really handsome, simple things …nothing too picketty," says Sallie. In her kitchen is a primitive wooden table made in a Northern New Mexican mountain village as well as a dipper and pail given to her by some gypsies from Spain. The red striped Navajo rug came from "Cozy McSparrons Trading Post" near the Four Corners.

left bottom

The long rifle and brass Blunderbust in the library's gun rack were carried by Sallie's ancestor when he was a runner for the Bank of England in London. Another gun she found "just laying under a tree in the middle of a forest in Oregon." A pueblo cradle swing is used to hold a heavy dictionary.

right

The adobe house was built and designed by Katherine Stinson Otero, the pioneer aviator who invented skywriting and was the first woman to do the "loop-the-loop" and to fly at night. Otero based the living room's proportions on the Golden Mean.

Schenck House

page 182
In the historic La Cienega neighborhood, near one of the stops on the old Camino Real, is the former home of J.B. Jackson, the renowned landscape designer. Jackson designed the terraced grounds and planted cottonwoods and a fruit tree orchard. Present owner, the subjective realist painter Billy Schenck, has very meticulously restored and renovated the "plantation pueblo" house.

above
Schenck rebuilt the library shelves and has placed his 1880's Mexican desk under the skylight. Turquoise blue Thomas Molesworth chairs with leather fringed upholstery are the very epitome of "cowboy high style" and were made in the 1940s.

right
The massive columns of the portal are almost twenty feet high and contain more than 1,000 adobe bricks apiece. The huge earth-toned jar sitting on a Navajo rug in the center of the oversized log table is the largest example known of its type: a Hohokam of the Santa Cruz phase.

left top

Chimayo blankets with a thunderbird design were woven specifically for the Molesworth chair and ottoman. Inspired by the Arts & Crafts movement, Thomas Molesworth experimented with leathers, burls, antlers, Indian weavings and cowboy artifacts in his funky Western furnishings.

left bottom

Acknowledging the tradition of East Coast wainscoting, Schenck has used two different shades of adobe muds on the walls of the dining room, one from the LaBajada area and one from Pojaque.

right

On the ledge of the living room's fireplace Schenck has displayed some of his favorite Anasazi pots. Billy, who says he is "an impassioned and totally addicted collector of prehistoric pots," has owned thousands of them. Frank Tenny Johnson did the luminous painting of two Navajo riders.

Nedra Matteucci

House and Garden

◀

page 188

A collection of santos *glows atop a richly carved Mexican altar in the entrance room of gallery owner Nedra Matteucci's house. The Canyon Road adobe is believed to have been built as early as 1768 and was first owned by Juan Jose Prada, a descendant of a Spanish army soldier from Chihuahua, Mexico.*

left top

An aspen-lined stone path leads to an old jacal shed in the Matteucci garden. Squared off cedar logs, more than thirty inches around, were set upright into the ground and then filled in with adobe to form this type of primitive building. This shed dates back to the late 17th century.

left bottom

The brick pretil, or coping, of the roof was added in the late 1800s by the artisans who built the St. Francis cathedral and is a classic Territorial feature. When former owner Margaretta Dietrich, a social activist and woman's suffrage leader from Nebraska, bought the house in 1927 she added rooms and connected two separate wings, but did not otherwise change the exterior's Territorial style.

right

A 1935 mural on the walls of the courtyard was painted by Margaretta Dietrich's sister Dorothy Stewart, who had been a student of Diego Rivera. The scene depicts the inside of a second class Mexican train. Nedra's friendly and very large pet pig, named Hamilton, resides in the courtyard now.

left

Nedra has built bancos on either side of the original fireplace in the living room, with spaces beneath them for storing firewood. Totemic figured slingshots from Guatemala line up on the mantel. The painting entitled "Eloise" is by Nicolai Fechin, a Russian painter who moved to Taos in the 1920s.

right top

The dining room, which now forms the connection between the two older wings of the house, contains a fireplace built by a Pueblo Indian woman in the 1920s. The columned Federal style mantelpiece was added on at a later date. A Moorish arch forms an elegant detail above a pair of wooden doors made by the WPA in the 1930s.

right bottom

Kachina figures stand in front of a landscape by contemporary artist Wilson Hurley in the sitting room. The carved radiator cover is another example of WPA work found throughout the house.

Virginia Dwan House

page 194

A rather dark and modest 1936 adobe off of Canyon Road was transformed by architect Laban Winger into a light-filled modern home for Virginia Dwan, a former art dealer from NY and LA. A portal and an open-beamed ramada were added onto the back of the house to open up the views. A carpet of gravel and selective plantings like lavender cut down on the amount of water needed to maintain a yard in the dry climate.

page 196

Laban Winger took the "inherent Santa Fe style of low ceilings and small windows" that came with the house and added more light by putting in the subtle clerestory skylight to one side of the pine-beamed living room ceiling. An antique carved angel's wing from Italy floats over the fat, round sculptural chairs whose arrangement speaks of the art of placement.

page 197

French doors were added to the very spare dining room for even more light and access onto the ramada. A rustic wood shelf set into a niche holds a painting done for Virginia by artist Sol Le Witt.

right

Dwan's very long, sunny and spacious art studio once housed an indoor swimming pool, added by previous owners in the 1980s. The arched skylights create a luminous dimension in which to work on paintings amid the rustic wood benches and tables.

Charlotte White House

former Vigil House

page 200

In 1958 Charlotte White and her late husband the sculptor Boris Gilbertson came upon the crumbling ruins of the Vigil House in the Barrio de Guadalupe, one of the oldest neighborhoods in Santa Fe. They immediately sensed the potential beauty of the place and undertook restoration, spending over twenty years of their "time, energy, and even money on this complete shambles." In this interior patio, they cleared away tons of debris and laid salvaged bricks in a beautiful flowing pattern.

left top

The guest bedroom was once a storeroom. Covers and pillows were brought back from one of Charlotte and Boris's motor trips to Mexico.

left bottom

A basket chair from the 1960s sits on the back patio. Many of Charlotte's garden flowers came from slips given to her by artist Olive Rush.

right

The couple at first camped out here in the sala because it was the most habitable part of the house. They found shards, flints and old adobe bricks dating back to the 1300s, indicating that the spot had been "a very old campsite for Indians long before the Spanish invasion." Boris Gilbertson, whose aim was always to "reveal something great in the commonplace," made many of the furnishings and sculptures in the room.

left

Charlotte painted the flowers on the kitchen door's windowpanes. This was often done in New Mexican churches to imitate stained glass. Doors and windows throughout the house were salvaged from a school that was torn down.

above

The wall of the inner placita *shows some of the old adobe bricks that date back to antiquity. The house was replastered by the expert hands of women from Cañones.*

T hanks to all the homeowners who were generous in allowing us to photograph their homes and to the following people for their help with the project:

The Cardwells
Anne Daley
Steve Earle
Eastman Kodak Company
Deanna Einspahr
Maria Fortin
Michael Fischer
Judy Geib
Dr. Mabel Ginsberg
Edith, Ernie & Nick Gross
Chris Hill
Terence McArdle at Kodak
David Morton
Aldo Sampieri
Kristen Schilo
Jonesey Stillstanding

Open to the public:

Randall Davey Audubon Center; for house tours
and information: 505 983 4609

Mabel Dodge Luhan Inn & Conference Center, Taos
For information & reservations: 800-846 2235

Index